50 The Essential Cookbook for Beginners

By: Kelly Johnson

Table of Contents

- Simple Scrambled Eggs
- Classic Pancakes
- Quick Stir-Fried Vegetables
- Beginner's Spaghetti Bolognese
- Easy Chicken Stir-Fry
- One-Pan Roasted Chicken
- Simple Beef Tacos
- Basic Tomato Soup
- Garlic Butter Shrimp
- Grilled Cheese Sandwich
- Easy Veggie Frittata
- Basic Chicken Salad
- Simple Grilled Vegetables
- Beginner's Homemade Pizza
- Quick Beef and Broccoli
- Basic Stir-Fry Noodles
- Simple Caesar Salad
- One-Pot Chili
- Easy Chicken Parmesan
- Classic Mashed Potatoes
- Simple Vegetable Soup
- Easy Egg Fried Rice
- Quick Beef Stew
- Homemade Meatballs
- Basic Homemade Burgers
- Easy Fish Tacos
- Simple Roasted Potatoes
- Basic Pesto Pasta
- Quick Veggie Stir-Fry
- Classic Beef Tacos
- Simple Chicken Quesadillas
- Quick Garlic Bread
- Beginner's Grilled Salmon
- Simple Veggie Pasta
- One-Pan Roasted Salmon

- Easy Chicken Soup
- Quick Veggie Wraps
- Basic French Toast
- Simple Veggie Burger
- Homemade Mac and Cheese
- Quick Rice Pilaf
- Easy Baked Ziti
- Simple Tuna Salad
- Easy Roasted Veggies
- Basic Omelette
- Simple Fruit Salad
- Easy Garlic Chicken
- One-Pot Spaghetti
- Quick Mushroom Risotto
- Simple Chocolate Chip Cookies

Simple Scrambled Eggs

Ingredients

- 4 eggs
- 2 tbsp milk
- Salt and pepper to taste
- 1 tbsp butter

Instructions

1. Whisk eggs, milk, salt, and pepper together until fully combined.
2. Heat butter in a non-stick pan over medium-low heat.
3. Pour in the eggs and cook gently, stirring occasionally until soft curds form. Serve immediately.

Classic Pancakes

Ingredients

- 1 cup all-purpose flour
- 1 tbsp sugar
- 1 tsp baking powder
- 1/2 tsp salt
- 1 egg
- 1 cup milk
- 2 tbsp melted butter

Instructions

1. In a bowl, whisk together dry ingredients.
2. In another bowl, whisk together egg, milk, and melted butter.
3. Combine wet and dry ingredients, stirring until just combined.
4. Heat a griddle or pan over medium heat, pour batter onto the pan, and cook until bubbles form, flipping to cook the other side. Serve with syrup.

Quick Stir-Fried Vegetables

Ingredients

- 1 cup broccoli florets
- 1 carrot, julienned
- 1 bell pepper, sliced
- 2 tbsp soy sauce
- 1 tbsp sesame oil
- 1 tsp garlic, minced

Instructions

1. Heat sesame oil in a pan over medium-high heat.
2. Add garlic and vegetables, stir-fry for 5-7 minutes until tender.
3. Stir in soy sauce and cook for another minute. Serve warm.

Beginner's Spaghetti Bolognese

Ingredients

- 1 lb ground beef or turkey
- 1 onion, diced
- 2 garlic cloves, minced
- 1 can diced tomatoes
- 1/2 tsp dried basil
- 1/2 tsp dried oregano
- 1/2 lb spaghetti
- Salt and pepper to taste

Instructions

1. Cook the ground meat in a pan over medium heat until browned.
2. Add onion and garlic, cooking until softened. Stir in tomatoes, basil, oregano, salt, and pepper.
3. Simmer for 15-20 minutes.
4. Meanwhile, cook spaghetti according to package instructions. Drain and toss with the sauce.

Easy Chicken Stir-Fry

Ingredients

- 2 chicken breasts, thinly sliced
- 1 bell pepper, sliced
- 1 carrot, julienned
- 2 tbsp soy sauce
- 1 tbsp hoisin sauce
- 1 tbsp olive oil
- 1 tsp ginger, grated

Instructions

1. Heat oil in a pan, add chicken, and cook until browned.
2. Add vegetables and stir-fry for 5-7 minutes.
3. Stir in soy sauce, hoisin sauce, and ginger, cooking for another minute. Serve hot.

One-Pan Roasted Chicken

Ingredients

- 4 chicken thighs
- 2 tbsp olive oil
- 1 tsp garlic powder
- 1 tsp paprika
- Salt and pepper to taste
- 2 cups potatoes, cubed

Instructions

1. Preheat oven to 400°F.
2. Rub chicken with olive oil, garlic powder, paprika, salt, and pepper.
3. Arrange chicken and potatoes on a baking sheet.
4. Roast for 35-40 minutes until chicken reaches 165°F.

Simple Beef Tacos

Ingredients

- 1 lb ground beef
- 1 packet taco seasoning
- 8 small tortillas
- Toppings: lettuce, cheese, salsa, sour cream

Instructions

1. Brown ground beef in a skillet over medium heat.
2. Stir in taco seasoning and a bit of water. Simmer for 5 minutes.
3. Warm tortillas and fill with beef mixture and desired toppings.

Basic Tomato Soup

Ingredients

- 1 can crushed tomatoes
- 1/2 cup vegetable broth
- 1/4 cup heavy cream
- 1/2 tsp dried basil
- Salt and pepper to taste

Instructions

1. Combine tomatoes and broth in a pot, bring to a simmer.
2. Stir in basil, salt, pepper, and cream.
3. Cook for another 5-10 minutes, then blend until smooth. Serve warm.

Garlic Butter Shrimp

Ingredients

- 1 lb shrimp, peeled and deveined
- 4 tbsp butter
- 3 garlic cloves, minced
- 1 tbsp lemon juice
- 1/4 tsp red pepper flakes

Instructions

1. Melt butter in a skillet, add garlic and cook for 1 minute.
2. Add shrimp, cook until pink and opaque, about 4-5 minutes.
3. Stir in lemon juice and red pepper flakes, serve immediately.

Grilled Cheese Sandwich

Ingredients

- 2 slices bread
- 2 tbsp butter
- 2 slices cheese (American, cheddar, etc.)

Instructions

1. Butter one side of each bread slice.
2. Place cheese between slices, buttered side out.
3. Grill in a skillet over medium heat for 3-4 minutes on each side until golden and the cheese is melted.

Easy Veggie Frittata

Ingredients

- 6 eggs
- 1/2 cup milk
- 1/2 cup bell pepper, diced
- 1/2 cup zucchini, diced
- 1/4 cup onion, diced
- 1/4 cup shredded cheese
- Salt and pepper to taste

Instructions

1. Preheat oven to 375°F.
2. Whisk eggs and milk together, then stir in vegetables, cheese, salt, and pepper.
3. Pour into a greased oven-safe skillet and bake for 20-25 minutes or until eggs are set.

Basic Chicken Salad

Ingredients

- 2 cups cooked chicken, shredded
- 1/2 cup mayonnaise
- 1 tbsp Dijon mustard
- 1/4 cup celery, diced
- Salt and pepper to taste

Instructions

1. In a bowl, combine shredded chicken, mayonnaise, mustard, and celery.
2. Season with salt and pepper, then mix well.
3. Serve on bread, crackers, or a bed of greens.

Simple Grilled Vegetables

Ingredients

- 1 zucchini, sliced
- 1 bell pepper, sliced
- 1 red onion, sliced
- 1 tbsp olive oil
- Salt and pepper to taste

Instructions

1. Preheat grill to medium-high heat.
2. Toss vegetables with olive oil, salt, and pepper.
3. Grill vegetables for 4-5 minutes on each side until tender and slightly charred.

Beginner's Homemade Pizza

Ingredients

- 1 pizza dough (store-bought or homemade)
- 1/2 cup pizza sauce
- 1 cup shredded mozzarella cheese
- Toppings: pepperoni, vegetables, etc.

Instructions

1. Preheat oven to 475°F.
2. Roll out pizza dough on a floured surface.
3. Spread pizza sauce, sprinkle cheese, and add toppings.
4. Bake for 10-12 minutes until the crust is golden and cheese is melted.

Quick Beef and Broccoli

Ingredients

- 1 lb beef sirloin, sliced thin
- 2 cups broccoli florets
- 2 tbsp soy sauce
- 1 tbsp hoisin sauce
- 1 tbsp sesame oil
- 1 garlic clove, minced

Instructions

1. Heat sesame oil in a pan, add garlic, and cook for 1 minute.
2. Add beef and cook until browned.
3. Stir in soy sauce, hoisin sauce, and broccoli. Cook until broccoli is tender. Serve over rice if desired.

Basic Stir-Fry Noodles

Ingredients

- 8 oz noodles (e.g., ramen or rice noodles)
- 2 tbsp soy sauce
- 1 tbsp sesame oil
- 1/2 cup mixed vegetables (carrots, bell pepper, etc.)
- 1 tbsp vegetable oil

Instructions

1. Cook noodles according to package instructions.
2. Heat vegetable oil in a pan, then add vegetables and stir-fry for 3-4 minutes.
3. Add cooked noodles, soy sauce, and sesame oil, stir to combine. Serve warm.

Simple Caesar Salad

Ingredients

- 4 cups romaine lettuce, chopped
- 1/4 cup Caesar dressing
- 1/4 cup croutons
- 2 tbsp grated Parmesan cheese

Instructions

1. Toss lettuce with Caesar dressing until evenly coated.
2. Top with croutons and Parmesan cheese. Serve immediately.

One-Pot Chili

Ingredients

- 1 lb ground beef or turkey
- 1 can kidney beans, drained and rinsed
- 1 can diced tomatoes
- 1 onion, diced
- 1 tbsp chili powder
- 1 tsp cumin
- Salt and pepper to taste

Instructions

1. Brown ground meat in a large pot over medium heat.
2. Add onion and cook until softened.
3. Stir in beans, tomatoes, chili powder, cumin, salt, and pepper. Simmer for 20-30 minutes. Serve with toppings such as cheese or sour cream.

Easy Chicken Parmesan

Ingredients

- 2 chicken breasts, breaded and cooked
- 1 cup marinara sauce
- 1/2 cup mozzarella cheese, shredded
- 1/4 cup Parmesan cheese

Instructions

1. Preheat oven to 375°F.
2. Place cooked chicken breasts in a baking dish.
3. Top with marinara sauce and mozzarella.
4. Bake for 15-20 minutes, until cheese is melted and bubbly. Serve with pasta.

Classic Mashed Potatoes

Ingredients

- 2 lbs potatoes, peeled and cubed
- 1/2 cup milk
- 4 tbsp butter
- Salt and pepper to taste

Instructions

1. Boil potatoes in salted water until tender, about 10-15 minutes.
2. Drain and mash with milk and butter until smooth.
3. Season with salt and pepper to taste. Serve warm.

Simple Vegetable Soup

Ingredients

- 2 carrots, sliced
- 2 celery stalks, chopped
- 1 onion, chopped
- 2 cloves garlic, minced
- 4 cups vegetable broth
- 1 can diced tomatoes
- 1 cup green beans, chopped
- 1 potato, diced
- Salt and pepper to taste

Instructions

1. Heat olive oil in a large pot over medium heat. Add onions, carrots, celery, and garlic. Cook for 5 minutes until softened.
2. Add broth, diced tomatoes, potatoes, and green beans. Bring to a simmer.
3. Simmer for 25-30 minutes or until vegetables are tender. Season with salt and pepper. Serve warm.

Easy Egg Fried Rice

Ingredients

- 2 cups cooked rice (preferably cold)
- 2 eggs, beaten
- 1/2 cup peas and carrots (frozen or fresh)
- 2 tbsp soy sauce
- 1 tbsp sesame oil
- 2 green onions, chopped
- 1 clove garlic, minced

Instructions

1. Heat sesame oil in a pan or wok. Add garlic and cook for 1 minute.
2. Add peas and carrots, and cook for 2-3 minutes.
3. Push the vegetables to the side, pour the beaten eggs into the pan, and scramble until cooked through.
4. Add the rice, soy sauce, and green onions. Stir-fry for 5 minutes. Serve warm.

Quick Beef Stew

Ingredients

- 1 lb beef stew meat, cubed
- 4 carrots, sliced
- 2 potatoes, cubed
- 1 onion, chopped
- 2 cloves garlic, minced
- 4 cups beef broth
- 1 tsp thyme
- Salt and pepper to taste

Instructions

1. Brown beef in a large pot over medium heat. Remove and set aside.
2. In the same pot, add onion and garlic and cook until softened.
3. Add broth, beef, carrots, potatoes, thyme, salt, and pepper. Bring to a boil.
4. Reduce heat and simmer for 45 minutes or until beef is tender. Serve warm.

Homemade Meatballs

Ingredients

- 1 lb ground beef or turkey
- 1/4 cup breadcrumbs
- 1/4 cup Parmesan cheese
- 1 egg
- 2 cloves garlic, minced
- 1 tsp Italian seasoning
- Salt and pepper to taste

Instructions

1. Preheat oven to 375°F.
2. In a bowl, mix all ingredients together.
3. Form into meatballs and place on a baking sheet.
4. Bake for 20-25 minutes until cooked through. Serve with marinara sauce and pasta or as an appetizer.

Basic Homemade Burgers

Ingredients

- 1 lb ground beef
- Salt and pepper to taste
- 4 burger buns
- Optional toppings: cheese, lettuce, tomato, pickles

Instructions

1. Preheat grill or skillet to medium-high heat.
2. Season ground beef with salt and pepper, and form into 4 patties.
3. Grill or cook the patties for 4-5 minutes per side, or until desired doneness.
4. Serve on buns with your favorite toppings.

Easy Fish Tacos

Ingredients

- 1 lb white fish fillets (like cod or tilapia)
- 1 tsp chili powder
- 1 tsp cumin
- 1 tbsp lime juice
- 1/2 cup shredded cabbage
- 1/4 cup sour cream
- Small tortillas
- Salt and pepper to taste

Instructions

1. Preheat oven to 400°F.
2. Season fish with chili powder, cumin, lime juice, salt, and pepper.
3. Bake fish for 12-15 minutes, or until flaky.
4. Assemble tacos by placing fish in tortillas, topped with cabbage and sour cream.

Simple Roasted Potatoes

Ingredients

- 4 large potatoes, cubed
- 2 tbsp olive oil
- 1 tsp garlic powder
- Salt and pepper to taste

Instructions

1. Preheat oven to 425°F.
2. Toss cubed potatoes with olive oil, garlic powder, salt, and pepper.
3. Spread potatoes on a baking sheet and roast for 25-30 minutes, turning halfway, until golden and crispy. Serve warm.

Basic Pesto Pasta

Ingredients

- 8 oz pasta
- 1/2 cup pesto sauce (store-bought or homemade)
- Parmesan cheese for topping

Instructions

1. Cook pasta according to package instructions.
2. Drain pasta, reserving 1/4 cup of pasta water.
3. Toss pasta with pesto sauce and reserved pasta water until well coated.
4. Top with Parmesan cheese and serve warm.

Quick Veggie Stir-Fry

Ingredients

- 1 cup bell peppers, sliced
- 1 cup broccoli florets
- 1/2 cup carrots, julienned
- 2 tbsp soy sauce
- 1 tbsp sesame oil
- 1 tsp ginger, grated
- 1 tbsp garlic, minced

Instructions

1. Heat sesame oil in a wok or pan. Add garlic and ginger, cooking for 1 minute.
2. Add vegetables and stir-fry for 5-7 minutes, or until tender-crisp.
3. Add soy sauce, stir to coat, and cook for 2 more minutes. Serve warm.

Classic Beef Tacos

Ingredients

- 1 lb ground beef
- 1 packet taco seasoning
- 1/4 cup water
- 8 taco shells
- **Toppings: shredded lettuce, diced tomatoes, cheese, sour cream, salsa**

Instructions

1. In a skillet, cook the ground beef over medium heat until browned.
2. Drain any excess fat, then add the taco seasoning and water. Stir to combine.
3. Simmer for 5-7 minutes until the mixture thickens.
4. Warm the taco shells according to the package instructions.
5. Spoon the beef mixture into the taco shells and top with your favorite toppings. Serve immediately.

Simple Chicken Quesadillas

Ingredients

- 2 cooked chicken breasts, shredded
- 4 flour tortillas
- 1 cup shredded cheese (cheddar or Mexican blend)
- 1/2 cup salsa
- 1 tbsp olive oil

Instructions

1. Heat olive oil in a skillet over medium heat.
2. Place a tortilla in the skillet, sprinkle with cheese, add chicken, and top with salsa.
3. Place another tortilla on top and cook for 2-3 minutes until the bottom is golden.
4. Flip and cook the other side for 2-3 minutes until golden and cheese is melted.
5. Slice and serve warm.

Quick Garlic Bread

Ingredients

- 1 loaf French bread
- 1/2 cup butter, softened
- 2 cloves garlic, minced
- 1 tbsp fresh parsley, chopped
- Salt to taste

Instructions

1. Preheat oven to 375°F.
2. Slice the French bread into thick slices and place on a baking sheet.
3. In a bowl, mix softened butter, garlic, parsley, and salt.
4. Spread the garlic butter mixture on each slice of bread.
5. Bake for 10-12 minutes or until golden brown and crispy. Serve warm.

Beginner's Grilled Salmon

Ingredients

- 2 salmon fillets
- 1 tbsp olive oil
- 1 tbsp lemon juice
- Salt and pepper to taste
- 1 tsp garlic powder

Instructions

1. Preheat the grill to medium heat.
2. Brush the salmon fillets with olive oil and lemon juice.
3. Season with salt, pepper, and garlic powder.
4. Grill the salmon for 4-5 minutes per side, or until cooked through.
5. Serve warm with lemon wedges.

Simple Veggie Pasta

Ingredients

- 8 oz pasta
- 1 cup cherry tomatoes, halved
- 1 cup spinach leaves
- 1/2 cup Parmesan cheese
- 2 tbsp olive oil
- Salt and pepper to taste

Instructions

1. Cook the pasta according to package instructions.
2. In a separate pan, heat olive oil over medium heat. Add tomatoes and cook for 3-4 minutes until softened.
3. Add spinach and cook until wilted.
4. Toss the cooked pasta with the veggies, Parmesan cheese, and season with salt and pepper. Serve warm.

One-Pan Roasted Salmon

Ingredients

- 2 salmon fillets
- 1 tbsp olive oil
- 1 lemon, sliced
- 2 garlic cloves, minced
- Salt and pepper to taste

Instructions

1. Preheat oven to 400°F.
2. Place the salmon fillets on a baking sheet lined with parchment paper.
3. Drizzle with olive oil and season with garlic, salt, and pepper.
4. Place lemon slices on top of the salmon.
5. Roast for 12-15 minutes or until the salmon flakes easily with a fork. Serve warm.

Easy Chicken Soup

Ingredients

- 2 chicken breasts, cooked and shredded
- 4 cups chicken broth
- 1 cup carrots, diced
- 1 cup celery, diced
- 1 onion, chopped
- 1 cup egg noodles
- Salt and pepper to taste

Instructions

1. In a large pot, bring chicken broth to a boil.
2. Add carrots, celery, and onion. Simmer for 10 minutes until vegetables are tender.
3. Add the shredded chicken and egg noodles. Cook for another 10 minutes until the noodles are tender.
4. Season with salt and pepper. Serve warm.

Quick Veggie Wraps

Ingredients

- 4 whole wheat tortillas
- 1 cup hummus
- 1 cup spinach leaves
- 1 cucumber, sliced
- 1/2 bell pepper, sliced
- 1/2 avocado, sliced

Instructions

1. Lay a tortilla flat and spread hummus in the center.
2. Layer with spinach, cucumber, bell pepper, and avocado slices.
3. Roll up the tortilla and slice into wraps. Serve immediately.

Basic French Toast

Ingredients

- 4 slices bread
- 2 eggs
- 1/4 cup milk
- 1/2 tsp cinnamon
- 1 tbsp butter
- Maple syrup for serving

Instructions

1. In a bowl, whisk together eggs, milk, and cinnamon.
2. Heat a skillet over medium heat and melt butter.
3. Dip bread slices in the egg mixture, coating both sides.
4. Cook on the skillet for 2-3 minutes per side until golden brown.
5. Serve with maple syrup.

Simple Veggie Burger

Ingredients

- 1 can black beans, drained and mashed
- 1/2 cup breadcrumbs
- 1/4 cup grated carrot
- 1/4 cup chopped onion
- 1 egg
- Salt and pepper to taste
- 4 burger buns

Instructions

1. In a bowl, mix the mashed beans, breadcrumbs, carrot, onion, egg, salt, and pepper.
2. Form the mixture into 4 patties.
3. Heat a skillet over medium heat and cook patties for 4-5 minutes per side, until golden.
4. Serve on buns with your favorite toppings.

Homemade Mac and Cheese

Ingredients

- 8 oz elbow macaroni
- 2 cups shredded cheddar cheese
- 1/2 cup milk
- 2 tbsp butter
- 1 tbsp flour
- Salt and pepper to taste

Instructions

1. Cook the macaroni according to package instructions.
2. In a separate pan, melt butter and whisk in flour.
3. Slowly add milk, stirring constantly until the mixture thickens.
4. Stir in cheese and season with salt and pepper.
5. Toss the cooked pasta in the cheese sauce. Serve warm.

Quick Rice Pilaf

Ingredients

- 1 cup rice
- 2 cups chicken or vegetable broth
- 1 tbsp butter
- 1 small onion, diced
- 1/2 cup frozen peas
- Salt and pepper to taste

Instructions

1. In a medium pot, melt butter over medium heat and sauté onion until translucent, about 3-4 minutes.
2. Add rice and stir to coat in the butter.
3. Pour in the broth and bring to a boil.
4. Reduce heat to low, cover, and simmer for 15-20 minutes until the rice is cooked and the liquid is absorbed.
5. Stir in the peas and season with salt and pepper. Serve warm.

Easy Baked Ziti

Ingredients

- 1 lb ziti pasta
- 2 cups marinara sauce
- 2 cups ricotta cheese
- 1 1/2 cups shredded mozzarella cheese
- 1/2 cup grated Parmesan cheese
- 1 tsp dried basil
- 1 tsp dried oregano

Instructions

1. Preheat the oven to 375°F.
2. Cook the ziti pasta according to package instructions.
3. In a large bowl, combine the cooked pasta, marinara sauce, ricotta, mozzarella, Parmesan, basil, and oregano.
4. Pour the mixture into a baking dish and top with extra mozzarella cheese.
5. Bake for 25-30 minutes, or until bubbly and golden. Serve warm.

Simple Tuna Salad

Ingredients

- 1 can tuna, drained
- 1/4 cup mayonnaise
- 1 tbsp Dijon mustard
- 1 tbsp lemon juice
- 1/4 cup chopped celery
- Salt and pepper to taste

Instructions

1. In a bowl, combine tuna, mayonnaise, mustard, lemon juice, and celery.
2. Mix until well combined.
3. Season with salt and pepper to taste. Serve as a sandwich filling or on a bed of greens.

Easy Roasted Veggies

Ingredients

- 1 zucchini, sliced
- 1 bell pepper, sliced
- 1 carrot, sliced
- 1 tbsp olive oil
- 1 tsp dried thyme
- Salt and pepper to taste

Instructions

1. Preheat the oven to 400°F.
2. Toss the vegetables with olive oil, thyme, salt, and pepper.
3. Spread in a single layer on a baking sheet.
4. Roast for 20-25 minutes, stirring halfway through, until the vegetables are tender and golden. Serve warm.

Basic Omelette

Ingredients

- 2 eggs
- 1 tbsp milk
- 1/4 cup shredded cheese
- Salt and pepper to taste
- 1 tbsp butter

Instructions

1. In a bowl, whisk together eggs, milk, salt, and pepper.
2. Heat a nonstick skillet over medium heat and melt butter.
3. Pour the egg mixture into the skillet and cook for 1-2 minutes, until the edges set.
4. Add cheese to one half and fold the omelette. Cook for another 1-2 minutes until the cheese melts. Serve warm.

Simple Fruit Salad

Ingredients

- 1 cup strawberries, sliced
- 1 cup blueberries
- 1 cup grapes, halved
- 1 orange, peeled and segmented
- 1 tbsp honey

Instructions

1. Combine all the fruits in a large bowl.
2. Drizzle with honey and toss gently.
3. Serve chilled.

Easy Garlic Chicken

Ingredients

- 2 chicken breasts
- 2 cloves garlic, minced
- 2 tbsp olive oil
- 1 tbsp lemon juice
- Salt and pepper to taste

Instructions

1. Preheat the oven to 375°F.
2. In a small bowl, mix olive oil, garlic, lemon juice, salt, and pepper.
3. Rub the mixture onto the chicken breasts.
4. Place chicken in a baking dish and bake for 25-30 minutes, or until the chicken is cooked through. Serve warm.

One-Pot Spaghetti

Ingredients

- 8 oz spaghetti
- 2 cups marinara sauce
- 2 cups water
- 1/2 onion, chopped
- 1 tsp dried basil
- Salt and pepper to taste

Instructions

1. In a large pot, combine spaghetti, marinara sauce, water, onion, basil, salt, and pepper.
2. Bring to a boil, then reduce heat to low and cover.
3. Simmer for 10-12 minutes, stirring occasionally, until the spaghetti is cooked and the sauce has thickened. Serve warm.

Quick Mushroom Risotto

Ingredients

- 1 cup Arborio rice
- 2 cups vegetable broth
- 1/2 cup mushrooms, sliced
- 1/4 cup Parmesan cheese
- 1 tbsp butter
- 1/4 cup white wine (optional)
- Salt and pepper to taste

Instructions

1. In a saucepan, heat the vegetable broth and keep it warm.
2. In a separate pan, melt butter over medium heat and sauté mushrooms until softened.
3. Add Arborio rice and stir for 1-2 minutes.
4. Slowly add warm broth, one ladle at a time, stirring frequently until the liquid is absorbed before adding more.
5. Once the rice is tender, stir in Parmesan cheese, salt, and pepper. Serve warm.

Simple Chocolate Chip Cookies

Ingredients

- 1 cup butter, softened
- 1 cup brown sugar
- 1/2 cup white sugar
- 2 eggs
- 2 1/4 cups all-purpose flour
- 1 tsp baking soda
- 1/2 tsp salt
- 2 cups chocolate chips

Instructions

1. Preheat the oven to 350°F.
2. In a large bowl, cream together butter, brown sugar, and white sugar.
3. Beat in the eggs, one at a time.
4. In a separate bowl, combine flour, baking soda, and salt. Gradually add the dry ingredients to the wet ingredients.
5. Stir in the chocolate chips.
6. Drop spoonfuls of dough onto a baking sheet.
7. Bake for 10-12 minutes or until golden brown. Serve warm.

www.ingramcontent.com/pod-product-compliance
Lightning Source LLC
LaVergne TN
LVHW081506060526
838201LV00056BA/2954